Louis Sachar

My Favorite Writer

Lily Erlic

WEIGL PUBLISHERS INC.

Published by Weigl Publishers Inc.
350 5th Avenue, Suite 3304, PMB 6G
New York, NY 10118-0069
USA
Web site: www.weigl.com

Library of Congress Cataloging-in-Publication Data

Erlic, Lily.
  Louis Sachar / Lily Erlic.
     p. cm. -- (My favorite writer)
  Includes index.
  ISBN 1-59036-288-8 (hard cover : alk. paper) -- ISBN 1-59036-294-2
(soft cover : alk. paper)
  1. Sachar, Louis, 1954---Juvenile literature. 2. Authors, American--20th
century--Biography--Juvenile literature. 3. Creative writing--Juvenile
literature. I. Title. II. Series.
  PS3569.A226Z65 2005
  813'.54--dc22

                                                    2004029930

Printed in the United States of America
1 2 3 4 5 6 7 8 9 0 09 08 07 06 05

Project Coordinator
Tina Schwartzenberger

Substantive Editor
Frances Purslow

Design
Terry Paulhus

Layout
Jeff Brown
Kathryn Livingstone

Photo Researcher
Kim Winiski

Contents

Louis Sachar

MILESTONES

1954 Born on March 20 in East Meadow, New York

1976 Graduates from the University of California at Berkeley

1978 Begins law school the same year *Sideways Stories from Wayside School* is published

1980 Receives law degree from Hastings College of the Law

1985 Marries Carla Askew

1987 Daughter, Sherre, is born

1989 Becomes a full-time writer

1999 Wins the Newbery Medal for *Holes*

2003 *Holes,* the movie, released in theaters

Do you know someone who makes up funny stories? Louis Sachar writes funny stories. Children laugh when they read his books. Once you begin reading his books, it is difficult to stop.

Louis went to school and studied to become a lawyer. His first book, *Sideways Stories from Wayside School*, was published during this time. Louis enjoyed being a lawyer, but he loved writing for children. At first, *Sideways Stories from Wayside School* did not sell well. Louis continued working in the lawyer's office. As soon as he could, he began writing full-time.

Most of Louis's stories are full of characters that make readers laugh. Louis Sachar has a good sense of humor and knows what children like to read. He creates **fictional** places and lifelike characters.

Early Childhood

Louis Sachar was born in East Meadow, New York, on March 20, 1954. He lived in New York until he was 9 years old. Louis's father worked as a salesperson in the Empire State Building. At the time, Louis thought it was "cool" that his dad worked in one of the world's tallest buildings. His mother, Ruth, worked as a real estate broker.

When Louis's family left New York, they moved to Tustin in Orange County, California. Every day, Louis walked through orange groves on the way to school. After school, he and his friends threw oranges at each other. Louis refers to himself as an "orange warrior" in his early years.

In 1643, East Meadow was just 1 square mile (17,000 acres) of plains around the settlement of Hempstead. East Meadow grew into a farming community, and later became a residential community.

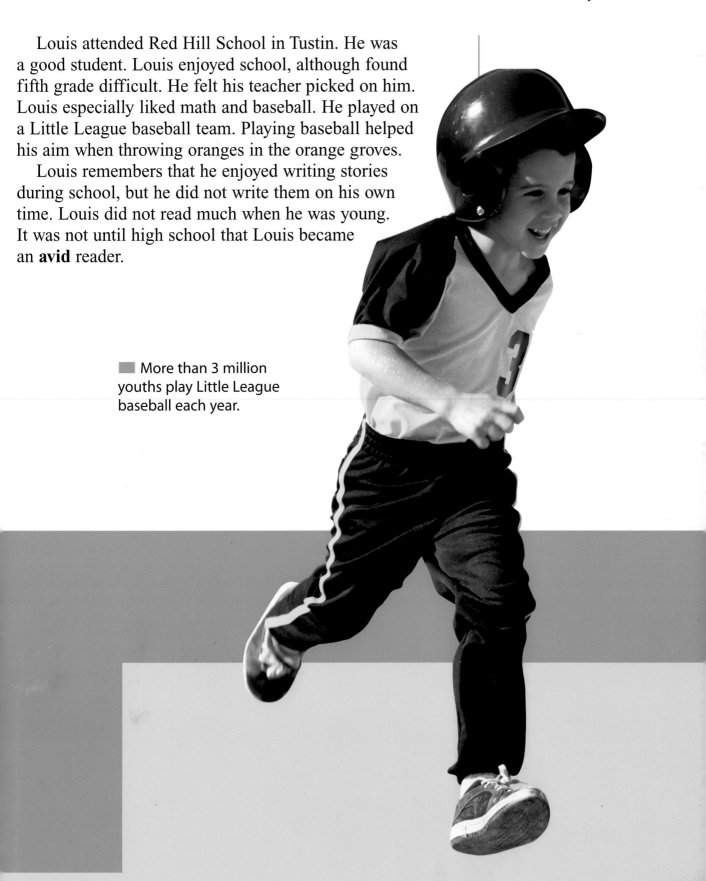

Louis attended Red Hill School in Tustin. He was a good student. Louis enjoyed school, although found fifth grade difficult. He felt his teacher picked on him. Louis especially liked math and baseball. He played on a Little League baseball team. Playing baseball helped his aim when throwing oranges in the orange groves.

Louis remembers that he enjoyed writing stories during school, but he did not write them on his own time. Louis did not read much when he was young. It was not until high school that Louis became an **avid** reader.

■ More than 3 million youths play Little League baseball each year.

Growing Up

Louis never thought that he would be a writer when he grew up.

While in elementary school, Louis never thought that he would be a writer when he grew up. His favorite subject was math. Louis received excellent grades and enjoyed solving math problems and puzzles.

In high school, Louis developed a love for reading. During his teen years, he had difficulty with school rules. Louis did not follow the rules. He dressed the way he wanted and grew his hair long. Even though teachers asked Louis to cut his hair and dress according to the rules, he refused. Louis's parents allowed him to break these rules.

After high school, Louis went to Antioch College in Ohio. He attended the college for 1 year. When his father died unexpectedly, Louis immediately returned to California to be near his mother.

$$12 \times 12 = 144$$

$$10 \times 10 = 100$$

$$1 \times 1 = 1$$

$$5 \times 5 = 25$$

Louis enjoyed math in school. Today, he visits schools and teaches students how to solve the math problems that appear in his books.

After his father's death, Louis did not return to college immediately. He accepted a job as a Fuller Brush Man. In the job, Louis went door-to-door selling household goods, especially brushes. Although he was a good salesman, Louis wanted to return to school. He went to the University of California at Berkeley, to study **economics**. Louis also took creative writing and English classes. He did not enjoy the English classes. Louis felt too much time was spent analyzing books. He decided to study Russian instead. It was difficult, and Louis grew frustrated. After 1 year, he decided to stop studying Russian.

Louis needed to take another course in place of Russian. He learned that he could receive college credits for working as a teacher's aide at a nearby elementary school. Louis became a lunch-break supervisor. He worked with children at Hillside Elementary School, where he was known as "Louis the Yard Teacher." This course became his favorite college class and a life-changing experience.

Inspired to Write

Louis Sachar's wife, Carla, and their daughter, Sherre, inspire some of his books. Many characters in Sideways Stories from Wayside School were based on real children Louis met when he worked at Hillside School.

Evans Hall is the second-tallest building on the University of California at Berkeley campus. Louis studied economics in this building.

Louis studied law in San Francisco. The city's Oakland Bay Bridge is the longest steel high-level bridge in the world.

The teacher's aide course was the most important class that Louis took in college. He loved spending time with the children in class and during the lunch break. Louis played games with them. He learned a great deal about them. Although Louis was paid only $2.04 a day, he thought that the course was worth his time.

Louis graduated from Berkeley in 1976. After graduation, he found a job in a sweater factory. Louis did not enjoy this job. Although he wrote in the evenings after work, Louis wanted more time to write.

Louis soon lost his job at the factory. He decided to return to school. Louis applied to Hastings College of the Law in San Francisco, California, even though his heart told him to become a full-time writer. Louis sent the manuscript for his first book, *Sideways Stories from Wayside School*, to publishers at the same time he applied to law schools. While Louis was in law school, his book was published.

Louis finished law school, passed the **bar exam**, and graduated. Although he was happy to pass the exam, Louis was not as excited as he thought he would be. While Louis was in school, he really wanted to write children's books. Louis found some time to write, but his dream was to write full-time. Soon, Louis found a job practicing law. Louis worked part-time to support himself while he wrote.

Louis married Carla Askew in 1985. Sherre, their daughter, was born in 1987. Throughout his career, Louis's wife and daughter have positively influenced his writing. Often, his wife and daughter inspire him. Sherre is happy that she is the first person to **critique** her dad's work. Carla helps Louis, too. The counselor in *There's a Boy in the Girls' Bathroom* is based on Carla.

In 1989, Louis stopped working at the law office and began writing full-time. His book, *There's a Boy in the Girls' Bathroom*, won many awards.

Louis practiced law for 9 years before he began writing full-time.

Favorite Authors

When Louis was young, he thought of his favorite authors as heroes. He wanted to be just like them. Louis's favorite children's author is E. B. White. Although he usually wrote for adults, E. B. also wrote children's books. His books include *Charlotte's Web*, *Stuart Little,* and *The Trumpet of the Swan*. Louis also enjoys reading Katherine Paterson's books. She wrote *Jacob I Have Loved*, *Bridge to Terabithia*, and *The Great Gilly Hopkins*. His other favorite children's authors include William Sleader, Walter Dean Myers, and Lois Lowry.

Learning the Craft

Louis thought that he could write stories that children would enjoy reading.

In high school, Louis loved reading. He read many books that helped his writing. For a creative writing class assignment, Louis wrote a story featuring a mean teacher named Mrs. Gorf. The teacher did not like the story and thought that Louis did not take the writing assignment seriously. Still, Louis liked the story.

When Louis worked as a teacher's aide during college, he realized he did not like the books that students were reading. Louis thought that he could write stories that children would enjoy reading. He wanted reading to be fun, not boring. When Louis showed his story about Mrs. Gorf to the children at Hillside School, they enjoyed it. Louis realized that he should write more stories for children.

Reading Damon Runyon's book, *In Our Town*, gave Louis the idea to write **vignettes**. He wrote *Sideways Stories from Wayside School*. The book is a collection of funny stories set at a school that is 30 stories high. The characters in the book are named after the students at Hillside School. He even named a character after himself—Louis the Yard Teacher.

Mrs. Gorf, a character in *Sideways Stories from Wayside School*, came from a story Louis wrote in high school.

After law school, Louis wrote *Johnny's in the Basement* and *Someday Angeline*. The books sold well, so Louis could spend more time writing.

Children all over the world love Louis's books. Many **reviewers** praise his writing. In 1989, Louis's books sold enough copies that he stopped practicing law and wrote full-time.

Louis continued to write books. Many of his books were translated into different languages. *Holes* is published in more than 20 countries, including Italy, Denmark, and the Netherlands. *There's a Boy in the Girls' Bathroom* is in bookstores in Japan and Italy. The Marvin Redpost series has had success in Germany and Italy. Louis likes the idea that his books have been published in different languages, even though he cannot read them.

Inspired to Write

William Goldman's *The Princess Bride* and Kurt Vonnegut's *Hocus Pocus* inspired Louis Sachar when he wrote the book *Holes*. The **style** of the two books influenced Louis. Louis read many books that helped him develop his own style.

Louis's book, *Holes*, was made into a movie in 2003. Louis wrote the screenplay for the movie.

Getting Published

Louis never thought his first book would be published. He sent his **manuscript** to ten publishers and waited for a response. One publisher decided to publish the book. Louis was excited, but *Sideways Stories from Wayside School* did not sell well when it was first published. Louis was not discouraged because he received many letters from children who enjoyed the book.

From the day Louis learned his book would be published, he struggled with his decision to attend law school. Louis questioned what to do with his life. Should he become a lawyer or an author? The answer became clearer when his books began selling well.

In 1982, Louis wrote his fourth book, *There's a Boy in the Girls' Bathroom*. Initially, he had trouble finding a publisher for this book. **Editors** said that the book had too many points of view. Two characters told the story. Editors thought that readers would grow confused and would not know which character was telling the story.

The Publishing Process

Publishing companies receive hundreds of manuscripts from authors each year. Only a few manuscripts become books. Publishers must be sure that a manuscript will sell many copies. As a result, publishers reject most of the manuscripts they receive.

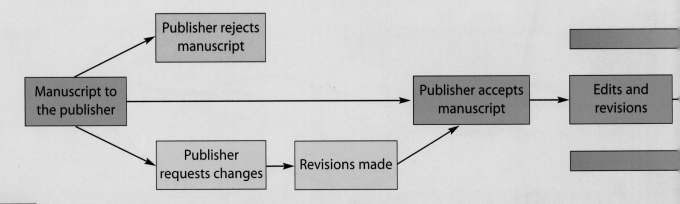

One publisher was interested in the book, but he wanted the book to be written only from the main character's point of view. Louis spent 2 hours every morning rewriting the novel. After many rewrites, he completed the novel. It was finally published in 1985.

While Louis rewrote *There's a Boy in the Girls' Bathroom* in the morning, he wrote *Sideways Arithmetic from Wayside School* in the afternoon. Louis wanted to help children realize that math could be fun. The book had many puzzles within its pages. Children found the puzzles tricky.

When visiting schools, Louis presented the book by writing the first puzzle on the chalkboard. He asked the children to solve the puzzle. Most children did not know what to do. Patiently, Louis showed the children how to solve the puzzle. When he presented the next puzzle, children responded by shouting out the answers.

Inspired to Write

Many of Louis's ideas come from adults or children he knows. Some ideas come from memories of when he was young. The themes in his books are humorous. He bases his **plots** on what children think about and what can happen to them.

Once a manuscript has been accepted, it goes through many stages before it is published. Often, authors change their work to follow an editor's suggestions. Once the book is published, some authors receive royalties. This is money based on book sales.

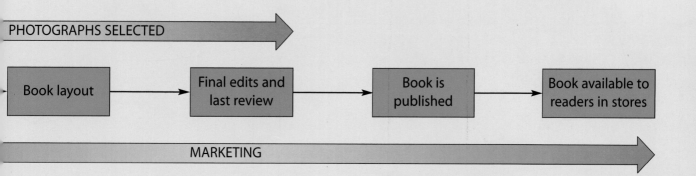

PHOTOGRAPHS SELECTED

Book layout → Final edits and last review → Book is published → Book available to readers in stores

MARKETING

Writer Today

Although Louis Sachar is currently writing another book, no one knows what it is about. He never talks about what he is writing to anyone, not even his wife. Louis believes if he does not talk about what he is writing, he is forced to write it down.

Louis has an office over the garage at his home in Austin, Texas. He loves his family life with his daughter, Sherre, and wife, Carla. His dogs, Lucky and Tippy, are a big part of his life, too.

Louis generally writes for 2 hours each day, first thing in the morning. Tippy knows when 2 hours have passed and it is time to take a walk. Tippy taps Louis on the shoulder to tell him. Only the dogs are allowed in Louis's office when he writes. They help him write by keeping him company. Lucky always sits by the door. Louis says if someone tries to come in, Lucky growls. "He seems to know that no one else is allowed in," says Louis. "Interruptions break the spell, and it's sometimes hard to get back."

■ Louis Sachar has received many awards, including the 1998 National Book Award for Young People's Literature. Louis received this award for *Holes*.

Louis often faces writer's block. When this happens, he has trouble writing. Louis cannot find the words to express himself or think of what will happen to the characters next. Still, Louis writes six **drafts** of a book. When he has writer's block, Louis simply tries to write anything down. He hopes to write it better in the next draft. Louis says that when he writes, he gets "a tremendous feeling of accomplishment from starting with nothing, and somehow creating a whole story and setting and characters."

Louis is busy every day. He loves taking his dogs for walks. His hobbies include the card game bridge and skiing. Every year, Louis and his family travel to Colorado to ski during the winter. During the hot Texas summers, they travel to places where the weather is cooler. California is a favorite place to visit to enjoy the beach.

Louis traveled to Austin, Texas, to accept the Texas Bluebonnet Award for *There's a Boy in the Girls' Bathroom*. The trip inspired Louis to move to Austin.

Popular Books

Louis Sachar is well known for his books for children ages 12 and under. His humorous stories have made children laugh and have kept them in suspense. Here are some of Louis's most popular books.

Sideways Stories from Wayside School

This book contains thirty stories about the children at Wayside School. The school was built 30 stories high, with one classroom piled on top of the other. The builder made a horrible mistake. There are many flights of stairs to climb because there is no elevator.

The first story is about Mrs. Gorf. Her classroom is on the top floor. Mrs. Gorf is a mean teacher who turns naughty children into apples. Eventually, she turns all of the students into apples except one. Jenny is about to be turned into an apple when she holds a mirror in front of herself. The magic reverses and hits Mrs. Gorf. The teacher turns into an apple. Then, Louis the Yard Teacher comes into the room. "Boy, am I hungry," says Louis. "I don't think Mrs. Gorf would mind if I ate this apple. After all, she already has so many." Louis eats the Mrs. Gorf apple.

The school is full of weird characters and wacky **antics** that are sure to make children laugh out loud.

There's a Boy in the Girls' Bathroom

Bradley Chalkers is the oldest boy in fifth grade. He sits in the last seat in the last row. No one wants to sit near him. The children in the class think he is an **outcast**. Bradley does odd things, such as cutting up his test paper into squares. He scribbles on paper during class. Bradley also tells lies.

At home, Bradley plays with his collection of little animal toys. Many of the animals are broken, but Bradley plays with them anyway. Ronnie, a little red rabbit with a broken ear, and Bartholomew, a brown-and-white bear standing on his hind legs, are Bradley's favorites. The animals are his friends.

Carla, a new school counselor, seems to like Bradley. Carla is encouraging. She believes that Bradley can change. Jeff Fishkin, a new student, also befriends Bradley. Still, when Bradley gets in a fight and receives a black eye, it seems as if no one wants to be his friend. Will Bradley have any friends? Can he start believing in himself?

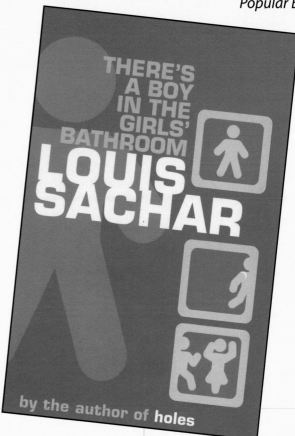

AWARDS
There's a Boy in the Girls' Bathroom

1990 Texas Bluebonnet Award

1990 Young Reader's Choice Award

Holes

Holes is a story about Stanley Yelnats. His last name is "Stanley" backward. One day, Stanley is walking down the street when a pair of stolen sneakers fall from the sky and land on him. The police arrest Stanley for stealing the sneakers. No one believes that the sneakers fell from the sky. The judge offers Stanley two choices. He can go to prison, or he can go to Camp Green Lake, a **correctional facility** for boys. Stanley chooses the camp.

"There is no lake at Camp Green Lake," is how the novel begins. The camp is in the dry, scorching Texas desert. The warden owns the only shade. She also has snake poison under her fingertips.

At Camp Green Lake, every day, each boy must dig a hole 5 feet (1.5 meters) wide and 5 feet (1.5 meters) deep. The warden makes the boys dig holes because she is looking for buried treasure.

Stanley meets other boys at the camp. Zero is quiet and digs quickly. He asks Stanley to teach him to read.

In exchange, Zero digs for Stanley. Magnet steals things. Squid pushes the other children around. Armpit smells bad. X-ray is the tough leader of one group of boys. ZigZag thinks there are small video cameras everywhere. Stanley's nickname is Caveman. Slowly, the boys become friends.

Marvin Redpost Series

Why Pick on Me?

Clarence, a student in Marvin Redpost's class, starts a rumor that Marvin Redpost is a nose picker. Marvin is the "biggest nose picker" in the entire school. Marvin's friends believe the rumor. Even his teacher believes the rumor. Everyone avoids Marvin. No one will talk to him. Marvin tries to prove his innocence.

Class President

Marvin's school has a special week. One day, everyone wears socks that do not match. Another day is "Vacation T-shirt Day." Wednesday is Hat Day. Thursday is Hole Day, when everyone wears their worst clothes to school. Even Marvin's teacher, Mrs. North, and the principal wear clothes with holes in them. Then, the principal learns that the president of the United States is coming to their school for a surprise visit. There is not enough time for anyone to change their clothes. Television crews and newspaper reporters arrive to film the president's visit. What will the students and teachers do?

A Flying Birthday Cake

Nick Tuffle has a sleepover to celebrate his birthday. Marvin lays in a sleeping bag outside with his friends. Marvin cannot sleep. The ground shakes, and Martin hears a humming noise. He sees something flying overhead. Is it a birthday cake? It looks green, like the frosting on Nick's birthday cake. Something glows on the cake, too. Marvin thinks it could be candles. Marvin stares at the sky all night. At least, he thought he stayed awake all night, but then he woke up in the morning. Was he dreaming, or did he really see a green birthday cake in the sky?

Creative Writing Tips

W riting novels, school reports, or short stories takes concentration. Sometimes it is difficult to create stories. These tips will help you write better.

Read

Louis suggests reading as many books as you can. If you read, then you can decide what you like about the books you choose. Reading a variety of books can help develop a sense of style. Reading helps build vocabulary and improves sentence structure. You can learn how to write by reading how others write.

Rewrite

Louis Sachar writes many drafts before he finishes a book. He rewrites his first draft because the ideas often do not flow together well. The second draft is better because Louis knows the characters and the plot. After many drafts, Louis sends his manuscript to the publisher. An editor works with Louis to make more changes to the novel. The novel is finished only when the rewriting is complete. Rewrite your work until the ideas and words flow together well.

Louis enjoys reading different types of books. When he finds an author he likes, he reads everything that author has written.

Research Other Writers

Louis has read books by his favorite authors many times. He researches what his favorite authors enjoy reading, so that he can read what they read. You can research what your favorite authors read and find the books in a library.

Brainstorming

Sit down with a piece of paper and a pen. Think about what you would like to write a story about. Write down the first word or idea that you think of. Draw a circle around the word. Continue writing down words and ideas as you think of them. Draw lines to connect the circles that have related words. Keep writing down words until you have enough ideas to create a short story. From the words, you can write sentences. This method is called brainstorming. Louis brainstorms ideas when he is writing his stories. He says, "I brainstorm until one idea leads to another which leads to another, and often it is the third or fourth idea which proves **salvageable**."

You can brainstorm ideas using a concept web. This web shows the main ideas in the first chapter of *There's a Boy in the Girls' Bathroom*.

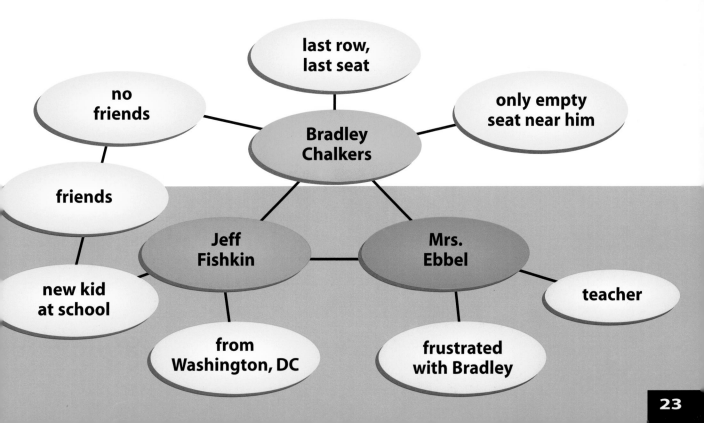

last row, last seat

no friends

only empty seat near him

Bradley Chalkers

friends

Jeff Fishkin

Mrs. Ebbel

teacher

new kid at school

from Washington, DC

frustrated with Bradley

Writing a Biography Review

A biography is an account of an individual's life that is written by another person. Some people's lives are very interesting. In school, you may be asked to write a biography review. The first thing to do when writing a biography review is to decide whom you would like to learn about. Your school library or community library will have a large selection of biographies from which to choose.

Are you interested in an author, a sports figure, an inventor, a movie star, or a president? Finding the right book is your first task. Whether you choose to write your review on a biography of Louis Sachar or another person, the task will be similar.

Begin your review by writing the title of the book, the author, and the person featured in the book. Then, start writing about the main events in the person's life. Include such things as where the person grew up and what his or her childhood was like. You will want to add details about the person's adult life, such as whether he or she married or had children. Next, write about what you think makes this person special. What kinds of experiences influenced this individual? For instance, did he or she grow up in unusual circumstances? Was the person determined to accomplish a goal? Include any details that surprised you.

A concept web is a useful research tool. Use the concept web on the right to begin researching your biography review.

- What did you learn from the book?
- Would you recommend the book to others?
- Was anything missing from the book?

- Where and when was the individual born?
- Describe the individual's parents, siblings, and friends.
- Did the person grow up in unusual circumstances?

- Where does the individual currently reside?
- Does he or she have a family?
- Does he or she have children or grandchildren?

Your Opinion

Adulthood

Childhood

REVIEWING A BIOGRAPHY

Main Accomplishments

Help and Obstacles

Work and Preparation

- What is the individual's life's work?
- Has he or she received awards or recognition for accomplishments?
- How have the person's accomplishments served others?

- What was the individual's education?
- What was his or her work experience?
- How does this person work; what is the process?

- Did the individual have a positive attitude?
- Did he or she receive assistance from others?
- Did the individual have a mentor?

Fan Information

Fans write many letters to Louis Sachar. They have written to him since his first book was published. When *Holes* won the Newbery Medal in 1999, readers were excited. In 2003, Walt Disney Pictures made the movie, *Holes*, based on Louis's book. Louis also wrote the **screenplay** for the movie. The movie characters reflect the characters in the book. When the movie was released in theaters, people became more aware of Louis's book and his talents. The movie is available on DVD.

Louis has visited many schools. He talks to children and teachers who have read his books. At book readings, Louis makes jokes and reads. Children and teachers ask him questions about his writing. Sometimes, Louis's school visits inspire story ideas.

Louis visits many schools to meet students and read from his books. He visited Lawrence Avenue Elementary School in Potsdam, New York, in 1999.

People who want to know more about Louis Sachar's books can visit his Web site. Many Web sites provide information about Louis's life and writing. To search for Web sites, type "Louis Sachar" into a search engine such as Google or Yahoo.

Louis Sachar

Louis Sachar is an award-winning author of over twenty fiction and educational books for children. Louis's most recent book, *Holes*, won the prestigious National Book Award and the Newbery Medal. For everything you ever wanted to know about Louis and his books, including the Marvin Redpost series and Wayside School series, follow the links below.

Go see HOLES, the movie, starring Sigourney Weaver, Jon Voight, and Shia La Beouf as Stanley Yelnats

MARVIN REDPOST SERIES

WAYSIDE SCHOOL SERIES

COMPLETE BOOKLIST

FAQ

AUTHOR BIO

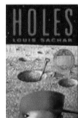

THE BOOK

THE MOVIE

WEB LINKS

Louis Sachar's Web site

www.louissachar.com

This Web site provides visitors with information about Louis Sachar. Fans can read his biography and learn about his books.

Holes

http://disney.go.com/disneyvideos/liveaction/holes/main.html

Visitors to this Web site can learn about the movie, *Holes*. They can even play a game and try to find Zero in the desert.

Quiz

Q: Where was Louis Sachar born?

1

A: East Meadow, New York

2

Q: Where did Louis Sachar live until he was 9 years old?

A: New York, New York

3

Q: From which university did Louis graduate?

A: The University of California at Berkeley

Q: What was Louis's favorite course at university?

Q: Which of Louis's books won the Newbery Medal?

A: Holes

A: A teacher's aide course

Q: When was his first book published?

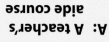

Q: Who is allowed in Louis's office when he writes?

A: His dogs, Lucky and Tippy

A: In 1978, during his first week of law school

Q: What is unique about the main character's name in *Holes*?

A: Stanley's last name is his first name spelled backward.

Q: What is Louis's daughter's name?

Q: Where do Louis and his family live today?

A: Sherre

A: Austin, Texas

Writing Terms

This glossary will introduce you to some of the main terms in the field of writing. Understanding these common writing terms will allow you to discuss your ideas about books and writing with others.

action: the moving events of a work of fiction

antagonist: the person in the story who opposes the main character

autobiography: a history of a person's life written by that person

biography: a written account of another person's life

character: a person in a story, poem, or play

climax: the most exciting moment or turning point in a story

episode: a short piece of action, or scene, in a story

fiction: stories about characters and events that are not real

foreshadow: hinting at something that is going to happen later in the book

imagery: a written description of a thing or idea that brings an image to mind

narrator: the speaker of the story who relates the events

nonfiction: writing that deals with real people and events

novel: published writing of considerable length that portrays characters within a story

plot: the order of events in a work of fiction

protagonist: the leading character of a story; often a likable character

resolution: the end of the story, when the conflict is settled

scene: a single episode in a story

setting: the place and time in which a work of fiction occurs

theme: an idea that runs throughout a work of fiction

Glossary

antics: pranks

avid: keen; eager

bar exam: a test taken to pass law school

correctional facility: a place where people who have broken the law are sent

critique: to offer an opinion

drafts: rough copies of something written

economics: the study of the way goods and wealth are produced, distributed, and used

editors: people who make changes in books

fictional: about characters and events that are not real

guild: a group of people with the same interests or goals

manuscript: a draft of a story before it is published

notion: idea

outcast: an outsider; someone left out of the group

plots: the order of events in works of fiction

reviewers: people who write their opinions about a book

salvageable: worth keeping

screenplay: outline or script of a movie

style: the way in which an author writes

vignettes: short stories told in a descriptive way

Index

Photo Credits

Cover: Bloomsbury
AP/AP Wide World Photo: pages 16, 26; Bloomsbury: pages 1, 3, 12, 18, 19, 21; Getty Images: pages 7 (AllSport Concepts), 8 (ImageSource), 10 (Imagebank), 11 (PhotoDisc Green), 17 (Imagebank); courtesy of HarperCollins Publishers: page 20; Steve McConnell: page 9 (Courtesy of University of California, Berkeley); Photos.com: page 22; Photofest: pages 13, 28; The Image Works: page 4.